THE CALM AFTER THE STORM

There is always life after the storm

By
NANA BEDIAKO BSN, RN, CCM

THE CALM AFTER THE STORM

Copyright © 2021 by NANA BEDIAKO BSN, RN, CCM

Unless otherwise noted, all Scripture references are from the King James Version of the Bible, copyright © 1979, 1980, 1982 by Thomas Nelson, Inc., Nashville, Tennessee.

Publisher
Royale Worldwide Publishing
www.royaleworlwidecorporation.com

First Edition
ISBN-13: 978-1-7322957-3-5 - E-book
ISBN-13: 978-1-7322957-4-2 - Paperback

Printed in the
United States of America

Publishing Consultants
Vike Springs Publishing Ltd.
www.vikesprings.com

For bookings and speaking engagements, contact us:
Royale Worldwide Corporation
Tel# +1 646-379-8246

Email: royaleworldwidecorp@gmail.com
Nana's books are available at special discounts when purchased in bulk for promotions or as donations for educational, inspirational and training purposes.

DEDICATION

This book is dedicated to Kwaku Kyei Mensah, my
lovely wife Linda, my daughters Jada and Eliana,
the CMIA family, all my friends and family,
and finally, you.

ACKNOWLEDGEMENTS

With deepest gratitude, I wish to thank every person that the Lord has brought into my life who has inspired, touched, and illuminated me through their presence, love, guidance and pristine advice.

My profound gratitude to Jeanette Kyei Mensah who saw this great potential in me and guided and pushed me beyond my limits to write my third book. Thank you, Apostle Alexander Gray, you told me years ago about this era of my life.

For generously contributing and sharing your wisdom, I appreciate you Apostle Dr. Kwabena Akufo, Rev. Asuo Mensah, Apostle Dr. Ami Narh, Rev. Arthur Bryant and Pastor Kwame Acheampong, Apostle and First Lady Shalders.

There is an African proverb that says, when you see a turtle on a fence, it certainly did not get there on its own. There are many people whom I can't even list that have made a tremendous impact on my life. Some have given me encouragement, spiritual guidance, advice, love and more.

To Apostle Oswald Boafo, thank you for your weekly advice; you saw great nuggets of spiritual gifts in me; I learnt great leadership and relational skills from you.

To Rev. Asuo Mensah, here is all the encouragement and mentorship you gave me through the years. Rev. Mark Asante Manu and Alexander Adu Gyamfi, you are always there through every milestone of mine, thank you. Thank you, Apostle Kwabena Akufo, Pastor George Aboagye.

To the members and leadership of Change Makers International Assembly Garfield New Jersey, the Apostolic Church USA, the Men's Movement, Witness Movement, all the Apostles, Pastors, Elders, Deacons and Deaconesses. Thank you all.

To Jesse Morgan, the Okharedia family, the Botchey family, Osekre family and all my ministry friends and colleagues, you have shown great love and support. You've been there through thick and thin. Love you all.

Team Bediako, thank you for your patience and for giving time off to take care of the Kingdom businesses.

Thank you Vike Springs Publishing Ltd., London UK for the professional comprehensive services - editing, proofreading, formatting/layout/design, worldwide publishing and distribution, printing and marketing.

Thank you Quick Graphix 951-530-1479 California for the cover design.

I thank God for these people whose knowledge, support and love directly or indirectly helped me immensely in writing this second book.

My parents Mr. & Mrs. Bediako, Mr. & Mrs. Kyei Mensah, Rebecca Aidoo, siblings: Vatraut , Victoria, Helmut and Afuah Kyei, Andrew Morgan and the

Acknowledgements

Morgan family, Yaw Gyasi, Emmanuel Barko Boafo, Pastor Nicholas Ankamah, Bishop Amo Brown, Apostle Ben Paul, my lovely big sister First Lady Kirby Assuo, Apostle Ami Narh, MOBA 95, Pastor Azigiza, Kwasi Koomson, Steven Donkor and team, Winifred Ekuban, Rev. & First Lady Shalders, Denise Robinson, Edinam Cudjoe, Linda Liverpool, Pastor Kwame Acheampong, Pastor Steve Paintsil, Pastor George Aboagye, Emmanuel Ntim, Gladys Adu, Joyce Mensah, Henry Ayensu, Ev. John Sena, Nana & Mrs. Asenso, Mr & Mrs Asenso.

Finally, my Heavenly Father, without you I am nobody.

TABLE OF CONTENTS

FOREWORD

Many years ago, one of our young adults performed an interpretive dance to the song "Alabaster Box" by CeCe Winans. This song chronicles the plight of and the actions of Mary who poured alabaster oil on Jesus' feet and wiped her feet clean with her hair as she wept (see John 12:1-8). Our young adult enacted the scene as real tears flowed from her eyes and she wiped the feet of one of boys acting as Jesus with her long hair. The scene was very moving and enthralling. Her act was not an act, but a demonstration of her own journey that was similar to Mary's.

Authenticity is facilitated by genuine identification. She identified fully with Mary and so her acting was authentic. So it is that you can't authentically speak about a storm if you have never been in a storm. This book arises out of the storms that peaked in the author's life not long ago. They have given Nana Bediako the authentic voice to speak on the subject.

His premise is biblically sound, based on the truth that every Christian goes through vicissitudes of life, with storms and a calm after the storm that inevitably leads to another storm. This book helps you to understand that along this journey of storms is the corresponding grace of God that sustains the believer. As Billy Graham has said, "The will of God will not take us where the grace of God will not sustain us."

Read this book to become equipped to go through the inevitable storms of life with the assurance that, "Weeping may endure for a night, but joy comes in the morning." (Psalm 30:5) Yes, there's life after the storm.

Blessings,
Apostle Dr. Kwabena Akufo

Chapter 1

THE PERFECT STORM

As the cloud gathers, we get a sense of possible rain. As the storm comes, there are uncertainties about what to expect; but we know that all things work together for our good (Romans 8:28).

In this book, we will learn how to walk through the intense storm and pick up the pieces after the storm passes. There are some things we can only learn in a storm.

When leaves change their color and fall to the ground, when the weather changes its temperature, everyone knows what season is coming.

"While the earth remaineth, seedtime and harvest, and cold and heat, and summer and winter, and day and night shall not cease." Genesis 8:22 KJV

Here are a few definitions of key terms that will lay the foundation for the discussion that follows in the rest of this book:

SEASON

The Oxford dictionary defines a season as a period of the year characterized by or associated with a particular activity or phenomenon. Time is defined as a plan, schedule, or an arrangement for when (something) should happen or be done.

There is a season and a time for everything under the sun, whether it is good or in your sight, bad, it's for a season and it will change. Nothing remains the same; summer, winter, autumn and spring always change. Seasons are temporary, so is crisis, the key to life is outlasting the season. If you can stay warm enough, summer will soon come. You don't quit or make a permanent decision in a season.

"1 To everything there is a season, and a time to every purpose under the heaven:

A time to be born, and a time to die; a time to plant, and a time to pluck up that which is planted;

A time to kill, and a time to heal; a time to break down, and a time to build up;

A time to weep, and a time to laugh; a time to mourn, and a time to dance"

Ecclesiastes 3:1-4 KJV

PURPOSE

The reason for which something is done or created, or for which something exists.

Characteristics of a SEASON

Seasons are not permanent, only God can be permanent.

Seasons gives HOPE – no matter how cold it is, SUMMER is coming.

Seasons allows us to plan for the future.

Seasons build FAITH – the just shall live by faith.

Our darkest seasons often have a lot to teach us, the most difficult times we encounter can become pivotal moments that can shape our lives. It's likely most people will or may have experienced some type of a loss, brokenness or pain. If you have been through a stormy season before, the second time around it feels different and one is able to handle it with more ease. The person that walked out of the storm is different from the one who first walked in.

I would like us to look at a few natural disasters and pandemics that have happened in the past. They are not permanent. Hurricanes, tsunamis, earthquakes and cyclones do not last forever. Here are some of the most devastating natural disasters of the 21st century:

Haiti Earthquake, 2010

In January 2010, one of the worst earthquakes ever recorded hit Haiti. The earthquake that struck west of the capital, Port-Au-Prince, measured 7.0 on the Richter scale with 52 aftershocks measuring 4.5 or greater.

It is estimated that 230,000 people died, 300,000 people were injured, and over one million were made homeless in one of history's most devastating natural disasters.

Indian Ocean Tsunami, 2004

In the early morning of December 26, 2004, an earthquake struck the Pacific sea floor, 150 miles off the west coast of the Indonesian island of Sumatra. The 9.0 magnitude earthquake quickly gave rise to a tsunami that within hours of the initial earthquake, hit the shorelines of Indonesia, Sri Lanka, India, Thailand, and the Maldives. More than 230,000 people were killed and millions were displaced.

Hurricane Katrina, 2005

The costliest and sixth deadliest hurricane ravaged the Gulf Coast of America in August 2005. Formed over the Bahamas, the hurricane crossed to southeast Louisiana as a Category 3 storm, causing destruction from central Florida to Texas. Over 1,800 people lost their lives.

Cyclone Nargis, 2008

At the end of April 2008, Cyclone Nargis hit Sri Lanka and Burma, causing widespread destruction. In Sri Lanka, the cyclone caused massive flooding and landslides, and in Burma it resulted in over 100,000 deaths. Overall, 150,000 people died in the cyclone and in its aftermath 50,000 went missing.

Let's look at other tragedies that are not natural disasters but impacted our world hugely, including pandemics and acts of terrorism:

The September 11 attacks (also referred to as 9/11) were the deadliest attacks on US soil since the Pearl Harbor bombing that launched the US into World War II. The event was a series of four coordinated attacks with planes as the main weapon. Two planes were flown into the twin towers of the World Trade Center in New York City, a third plane hit the Pentagon just outside Washington, D.C., and the fourth plane crashed in a field in Shanksville, Pennsylvania. The attack resulted in about 3000 fatalities and over 25,000 injuries and substantial long-term health consequences in addition to at least $10 billion in infrastructure and property damage.

On May 9th, 2001, Ghana experienced the worst tragedy in African sporting history – the deaths of at least 126 fans and hundreds injured in a stampede at a football match in the capital, Accra. It was a day where fathers, mothers, sisters, brothers and even children left their homes on a beautiful Sunday afternoon to go support their soccer teams, but at the end of the day, loved ones were at the morgue to identify their family members.

The world has experienced many pandemics and epidemics through the years like the plague, cholera, all kinds of flu, Ebola and Coronavirus just to mention a few. These health crises took the lives of millions of people worldwide. I will focus on the Covid-19 pandemic which is a type of storm or crisis.

As we reflect on the horrible images of the storm's aftermath, what would you say has been the worst day of your life? Maybe it was the day a beloved family member died. Perhaps it was a day you fell off a financial tightrope, and found there was no safety net. Or possibly a day of the discovery of a disease, an arrest, a divorce, a lawsuit, an attack... You fill in the blank.

If you've lived long enough, you've seen such a day. It's the nature of unexpected storms. The unexpected storm is a part of life. A few weeks ago, I lost a wonderful man who was like a father to me; he loved and cared so much about me. On the day he was called home, I spoke with him about an hour before he passed. There was no sign that it would be the last time I would be speaking with him.

2020 was a year of great excitement for our church; God gave us a theme which we titled "Our year of Uncommon Harvest." However, the year started with tremendous ups and downs; unexpected news, tragedies, loss of jobs and the season of Covid-19 which was unprecedented and affected everyone.

Jesus and his disciples encountered many unexpected moments. Some of those moments were very difficult.

Matthew, who lived through the storm, tells us what happened in his account below:

Matthew 8:23-27

"23 And when he was entered into a ship, his disciples followed him.

24 And, behold, there arose a great tempest in the sea, insomuch that the ship was covered with the waves: but he was asleep.

25 And his disciples came to him, and awoke him, saying, Lord, save us: we perish.

26 And he saith unto them, Why are ye fearful, O ye of little faith? Then he arose, and rebuked the winds and the sea; and there was a great calm.

27 But the men marveled, saying, What manner of man is this, that even the winds and the sea obey him!"

After Jesus got into a boat and His disciples followed Him, suddenly without warning, a furious storm came up on the lake, and the waves swept over the boat. But Jesus was sleeping. The disciples went and woke him, saying, "Lord, save us! We're going to drown!"

He replied, "You of little faith, why are you so afraid?" Then he got up and rebuked the winds and the waves, and it was completely calm.

The men were amazed and asked, "What kind of man is this? Even the winds and the waves obey him!"

The phrase that strikes me here is ... "without warning." It was a normal day, business as usual. And without warning, it was all at risk. It became imperative for the people in the boat to stay alive. That's all. Just stay alive. To be prepared is better than getting caught by surprise. Given that the disciples didn't get a free pass out of storms, then the rest of us who follow Jesus shouldn't expect life to be much different.

Do you agree with me that, even if one is walking with Jesus, the son of the living God, they can still encounter distress? Or do you think that if a person gives up everything to follow Jesus, He would make sure they never had to face any difficulties? Like any good employer would try to do, Jesus would make sure that his workers had a stress-free environment in which they could perform their tasks to obtain the maximum results.

On this Christian journey, no one gets a free pass from funerals, disease or tragedy. You don't get to bypass disappointment just because you are faithful in following Jesus. There's no guarantee of good times, if you'll just be a good disciple.

At some point in life, it would be a good idea if you came to grips with one of the most basic truths of life: Death is a part of life. Death happens. It's as certain as birth, and a lot more certain than taxes. I find far too many Christians acting as if they somehow believed they would never die. I find far too many Christians stunned by their approaching demise, shocked that an aging loved one might be taken from them, just speechless by the reality that if you live long enough, you're going to have to go to some funerals that hurt.

One of the most difficult parts of my young ministry life was the loss of one of our founding pillars of Change Makers International Assembly of the Apostolic Church, Kwaku Kyei Mensah who was a father of the church. What any young pastor does not anticipate is to bury a member. When it happened to me, I went to the Lord in prayer; questioned God, did not know what to share with the congregation, but I saw the Lord. The Lord gave me a word for the congregation which was for us to be thankful for the years He (God) gave life to His servant, and to remember and celebrate his life. What will you be remembered for when you leave this earth? Just ponder over this for a minute. Can we say what Paul boldly professed in

2 Timothy 4:7-8(KJV)

"7 I have fought a good fight, I have finished my course, I have kept the faith:

8 Henceforth there is laid up for me a crown of righteousness, which the Lord, the righteous judge, shall give me at that day: and not to me only, but unto all them also that love his appearing."

As believers we need to be confident not only in this life alone, but also have hope in eternal life. I get moved by what Paul said in 1 Corinthians 15:19 (KJV): "If in this life only we have hope in Christ, we are of all men most miserable." Why will one be "most miserable?"

Shunning evil, the worldly enjoyment, all the evil deeds; the time you spend going to church, working in the house of God; the financial support and all the sacrifices you've made; and to have no assurance of going to heaven – that will really be a miserable encounter.

God is in control

One thing I noticed in all the eye-witness reports of those who experienced these storms is that people felt completely out of control. Witnesses in an earthquake-rumbled area found themselves unable to stand, unable to lean on anything for support, unable to hold the cameras steady, just completely out of control.

There was nothing they could hold on to for support. When life gives you a big enough crisis, you need something that isn't moving.

Something that isn't shaking. Something that isn't capable of letting you down. You need the anchor that keeps the soul and His name is Jesus. Jesus is the one you want to know when life starts getting hit by one storm after another.

Jesus was obviously in control when the storm came on the Sea of Galilee. He was sleeping in the midst of the storm. Can you imagine sleeping through an earthquake, tsunami or cyclone? No one sleeps through this kind of disaster. Jesus was so relaxed that the disciples had to wake Him. And when He finally spoke, He asked them a most unusual question: "Where is your faith? Why are you so afraid?" Hmm, how many people wouldn't be afraid of drowning at sea? A capsizing boat is not an experience anyone would love to have.

There are many kinds of storms; your storm might not be an earthquake, it might be dealing with barrenness, a newly diagnosed cancer with a time ticking prognosis, the loss of a loved one, loss of a job, a breakup of your church, divorce, bankruptcy and more. If you are going through such a storm, Jesus is asking you, where is your faith? And why are you afraid?

Jesus is always in control. Watching everything Jesus did, John came to a point where he said in,

John 1:3

"All things were made by him; and without him was not anything made that was made."

Paul thought about the life of Jesus for years, and finally wrote this sentence in Colossians 1:17:

"And he is before all things, and by him all things consist." And when Jesus said to the storm: "Be still!", the storm simply obeyed. Peace is always stronger and more powerful than any storm. Are you in a storm? Know that Jesus is in control. Whether or not the earth is shaking or life as you know it is changing rapidly, be assured that Jesus is in control. I would definitely feel very comfortable getting in a boat with the one who is in control.

The disciples surviving the storm at sea was possible only because Jesus was in the boat. They tried all their skills at surviving, and it just wasn't enough. But because Jesus was in the boat, they survived with ease. There was a lot the disciples learned from this experience, which was the fact that Jesus was really in control.

The key to surviving life's storms – all the unexpected things that can toss us around – is having a personal relationship with Jesus Christ. As surely as the disciples needed to be in the boat with Jesus, you've got to have a living, breathing, intimate relationship with Jesus.

Mark 6:45-52

"45 Immediately Jesus made his disciples get into the boat and go on ahead of him to Bethsaida, while he dismissed the crowd.

46 After leaving them, he went up on a mountainside to pray.

47 Later that night, the boat was in the middle of the lake, and he was alone on land.

48 He saw the disciples straining at the oars, because the wind was against them. Shortly before dawn he went out to them, walking on the lake. He was about to pass by them,

49 but when they saw him walking on the lake, they thought he was a ghost. They cried out,

50 because they all saw him and were terrified. Immediately he spoke to them and said, 'Take courage! It is I. Don't be afraid.'

51 Then he climbed into the boat with them, and the wind died down. They were completely amazed,

52 for they had not understood about the loaves; their hearts were hardened."

Mark writes about another sea encounter where the disciples were faced with another storm. Jesus instructed the disciples to get into a boat at night and travel across the sea to Bethsaida. In their obedience to Jesus, the disciples ran directly into a storm.

Their obedience literally took them into the nucleus of a disaster. Have you ever been in a situation where doing the right thing or obeying God lands you in an uncomfortable situation where you wonder if God is really with you or against you? He did assure us that He will never leave us nor forsake us, however we sometimes find it difficult to believe this word when we are faced with a storm.

I wish I could tell you that following Jesus means you will never have to face any storm. I wish I could tell you that following Jesus means that the waters of life will always be calm. I wish I could tell you that following Jesus means life will be rosy and all of your days sweet. But I can't.

The disciples were following Jesus, and they ran right into rough seas. The disciples discovered, as many of us have also discovered that you can be both in the center of God's will, and still in a storm. Just make sure you are always seeing Jesus in the storm and not focusing all your energy on the storm.

Our Christian walk with Jesus doesn't offer immunity from troubles. What it does give is the opportunity to experience Him and His faithfulness in the midst of the storm.

This life is a journey that is sometimes filled with troubles, regardless of whether or not you follow Jesus. One has the choice to allow Jesus to be with you when you go through the storm or to decide to go through them alone.

Always remember that though we may go through the valley of the shadow of death, Jesus is with us. You are not alone. And, rather than focus on the problems, focus on the promises of God.

If you focus too much on the problems, you will lose sight of the promises. Fix your eyes on Jesus and His Word and He will bring peace and calm to the struggles you are facing.

God always has a purpose in our pain. He doesn't always reveal it when we want Him to. In some cases, we won't discover what it is until we get to Heaven. Romans 8:28 says, "And we know that in all things God works for the good of those who love him, who have been called according to his purpose."

When you feel like giving up, look up. Fix your hope on Him.

Chapter 2

IT'S INTENTIONAL

An evil spirit from the Lord:

1 Samuel 16:12-23

"12 So he sent for him and had him brought in. He was glowing with health and had a fine appearance and handsome features. Then the Lord said, 'Rise and anoint him; this is the one.'

13 So Samuel took the horn of oil and anointed him in the presence of his brothers, and from that day on the Spirit of the Lord came powerfully upon David. Samuel then went to Ramah.

David in Saul's Service

14 Now the Spirit of the Lord had departed from Saul, and an evil spirit from the Lord tormented him.

15 Saul's attendants said to him, 'See, an evil spirit from God is tormenting you.

16 Let our lord command his servants here to search for someone who can play the lyre. He will play when the evil spirit from God comes on you, and you will feel better.'

17 So Saul said to his attendants, 'Find someone who plays well and bring him to me.'

18 One of the servants answered, 'I have seen a son of Jesse of Bethlehem who knows how to play the lyre. He is a brave man and a warrior. He speaks well and is a fine-looking man. And the Lord is with him.'

19 Then Saul sent messengers to Jesse and said, 'Send me your son David, who is with the sheep.'

20 So Jesse took a donkey loaded with bread, a skin of wine and a young goat and sent them with his son David to Saul.

21 David came to Saul and entered his service. Saul liked him very much, and David became one of his armor-bearers.

22 Then Saul sent word to Jesse, saying, 'Allow David to remain in my service, for I am pleased with him.'

23 Whenever the spirit from God came on Saul, David would take up his lyre and play. Then relief

would come to Saul; he would feel better, and the
evil spirit would leave him."

These scriptures do not say God was an evil spirit.
However, when evil comes, God is in control. Often
God will even use evil to convey good. Romans 8:28-
"and we know that all things will work together for
good to them who love God and those who are called
according to His purpose." Even bad things will work
together for our good.

God monitors how much evil there is each day.
His hand is on the thermostat and turns it how He
wants. Job makes me understand, unless God gives
the permission, the devil cannot attack a child of God.
We are hidden in Christ and Christ in God. (Colossians 3:3)

If God allows evil to come my way, then it will
ultimately work together for my good. When Samuel
anointed David as king, Saul was still on the throne,
but the spirit of God had already departed from him.
Saul was not God's choice but became God's instrument for His choice.

God is able to use the conditions, storms, crises or
adversities you are going through to create an atmo-
sphere of bringing His purpose into your life. He will
allow evil to come in when you are too comfortable
with where you are now or use it to catapult you into
His plans for your life.

In Proverbs 18:16 the Bible says, "a man's gift
makes room for him, and brings him before great
men." Every creation is for a purpose, and the creator

of the thing knows the purpose. We are not on this earth by chance or mistake. God has deposited unique gifts in us which will bring to pass our destiny.

Let's look at the scripture in the Book of 1 Samuel 16 to understand that nothing just happens to a child of God:

"14 Now the Spirit of the Lord had departed from Saul, and an evil spirit from the Lord tormented him.

15 Saul's attendants said to him, 'See, an evil spirit from God is tormenting you.

16 Let our lord command his servants here to search for someone who can play the lyre. He will play when the evil spirit from God comes on you, and you will feel better.'"

God had blessed David with the gift of playing the lyre (a stringed instrument like a small U-shaped harp with strings fixed to a crossbar, used especially in ancient Greece) very skillfully. There is no coincidence in the vocabulary of God, it's all intentional. It was not a coincidence for the evil spirit to torment Saul, and for the only remedy to be the soothing music of lyre; and David was on the list for the best player in town.

Don't forget that David had at this time been anointed king by Samuel and God needed him to have access to the palace and get himself acclimated to the place where he would take over in the future. The evil spirit tormenting Saul created a position of employment in the palace for David. If David had prayed for Saul to be healed, he probably would not have had the opportunity to work in the palace.

In verses 21 and 22, David came to Saul and entered his service. Saul liked him very much, and David became one of his armor-bearers. "22 Then Saul sent word to Jesse, saying, 'Allow David to remain in my service, for I am pleased with him.'"

The journey that led David into the palace was the result of a crisis, but it was intentional. The process also molded David into what God had predestined for him. David later faced many challenges, but it all worked out for his good. If you come out of a storm, you won't be the same person who walked into it; there is a purpose in every storm.

The intentions of God for Job

Job 1:1-3,6-22

"1 In the land of Uz there lived a man whose name was Job. This man was blameless and upright; he feared God and shunned evil.

2 He had seven sons and three daughters,

3 and he owned seven thousand sheep, three thousand camels, five hundred yoke of oxen and

five hundred donkeys, and had a large number of servants. He was the greatest man among all the people of the East.

6 One day the angels came to present themselves before the Lord, and Satan also came with them.

7 The Lord said to Satan, 'Where have you come from?' Satan answered the Lord, 'From roaming throughout the earth, going back and forth on it.'

8 Then the Lord said to Satan, 'Have you considered my servant Job? There is no one on earth like him; he is blameless and upright, a man who fears God and shuns evil.'

9 'Does Job fear God for nothing?' Satan replied.

10 'Have you not put a hedge around him and his household and everything he has? You have blessed the work of his hands, so that his flocks and herds are spread throughout the land.

11 But now stretch out your hand and strike everything he has, and he will surely curse you to your face.'

12 The Lord said to Satan, 'Very well, then, everything he has is in your power, but on the man himself do not lay a finger.' Then Satan went out from the presence of the Lord.

13 One day when Job's sons and daughters were feasting and drinking wine at the oldest brother's house,

14 a messenger came to Job and said, 'The oxen were plowing and the donkeys were grazing nearby,

15 and the Sabeans attacked and made off with them. They put the servants to the sword, and I am the only one who has escaped to tell you!'

16 While he was still speaking, another messenger came and said, 'The fire of God fell from the heavens and burned up the sheep and the servants, and I am the only one who has escaped to tell you!'

17 While he was still speaking, another messenger came and said, 'The Chaldeans formed three raiding parties and swept down on your camels and made off with them. They put the servants to the sword, and I am the only one who has escaped to tell you!'

18 While he was still speaking, yet another messenger came and said, 'Your sons and daughters were feasting and drinking wine at the oldest brother's house,

19 when suddenly a mighty wind swept in from the desert and struck the four corners of the house. It collapsed on them and they are dead, and I am the only one who has escaped to tell you!'

20 At this, Job got up and tore his robe and shaved his head. Then he fell to the ground in worship

21 and said: 'Naked I came from my mother's womb, and naked I will depart.

The Lord gave and the Lord has taken away; may the name of the Lord be praised.'

22 In all this, Job did not sin by charging God with wrongdoing."

We serve a God who knows our end from the beginning. He is the Alpha and Omega, the omnipotent and omniscient; the creator of the universe, and the all-knowing God. How can anyone try to compete with such a God? Satan should have been smart and known that His actions were intentional or a setup for increase.

In Chapter 1 of the Book of Job, we read that Job was a man who tried to do things right. He was a blameless person who avoided evil and made sacrifices for his children. Even though he tried to do everything right, all of a sudden everything went bad for him.

- All of his beautiful children died.
- His marriage became miserable and sour.
- His wife started talking foolishly and discouraged him.
- Job went from being in excellent health to bad.
- He went from prosperity to poverty.
- He had sores from the top of his head to the bottom of his feet.

Here is a man who lived a righteous life, tried to do everything right but everything went wrong for him. Job is the epiphany of the phrase "bad things can happen to good people and good things happen to bad people."

In the Book of Job, two chapters of great faith are followed immediately by 35 chapters of great questions. Job wasn't alone with his questions. Do you ever ask God questions when you go through trials? During this season of the Covid-19 pandemic, there have been many questions that have evolved.

Jeremiah couldn't preach without weeping, questioning how God could have allowed such despair.

David struggled with questions for years, especially while hiding from Saul and wondering if he'd even live to see the reign the prophet had said would be his. Remember how he began his Psalm 13?

"How long, O LORD? Will you forget me forever?

How long will you hide your face from me?"

Paul wasted two years in a prison cell in Caesarea, right in the middle of his best church-planting days. Maybe that's where he learned that the Holy Spirit would take over his desperate prayers, when he had run out of painful words.

Romans 8:26-27: "In the same way, the Spirit helps us in our weakness. We do not know what we ought to pray for, but the Spirit himself intercedes for us with groans that words cannot express. And he who searched our hearts knows the mind of the Spirit, because the Spirit intercedes for the saints in accordance with God's will."

The questions about suffering even reached the mouth of Jesus, as he genuinely wrestled with the internal agony before the crucifixion. "Must I really do this?" he asked; under such stress that blood vessels popped in his forehead. "Is there no other way?" (See Luke 22:42-43)

Surviving a storm or any crisis depends on your support system. There are many kinds of friends or family. I have experienced very few friends who have been with me through thick and thin. Some friends will only show their loyalty when they are with you behind closed doors but will not defend you in public. There are those who will only show up when things are good and those who will only show up when you have a problem. Who are true friends?

Let's look at Job's friends and his wife.

They started out well. They sat with him in silence, sharing his suffering. They offered a comforting presence, and if they had stopped there they would've been seen as a very compassionate group of friends.

But they couldn't leave well enough alone; they had to evaluate Job's suffering. When we know of people who are hurting, we need to be slow to speak and quick to listen. We need to bear their burdens and offer comfort. We need not "explain" their pain. Sometimes those closest to you can even cause you more agony in the midst of the storm. This is what Job's wife said to him, "'Are you still maintaining your integrity? Curse God and die!' 10 He replied, 'You are talking like a foolish woman. Shall we accept good from God, and not trouble?'" (Job 2:9-10)

While Job was going through these trials, he felt that God was not answering all the questions he had about his dilemma.

After 37 chapters of silence, God finally answered Job in Job 38 (you can read the whole chapter). God spoke to Job out of a mighty storm to impress Job with His infinite power. Job wanted to know the answers but God refused to give them.

Job 38:1-4

"1 Then the Lord spoke to Job out of the storm. He said:

2 'Who is this that obscures my plans with words without knowledge?

> 3 Brace yourself like a man;
> I will question you,
> and you shall answer me.

> 4 Where were you when I laid the earth's
> foundation?

> Tell me, if you understand."'

Instead of giving him the answers he wanted, God assured Job that He was in control and that He alone knew the reason for Job's suffering. God taught Job that it is better to know God than to know all the answers. That can be hard to accept when we want to know all the answers. Job learned the hard lesson that when everything is stripped from our lives, all we have is God. During this Covid-19 pandemic, the world came to the realization that it will only take God. The world lost hope and had to look up unto God alone.

Like Job, suffering tests our faith. Suffering can strengthen our faith or suffering can shatter our faith. We will have to make the choice: Suffering will either drive us into God's arms or cause us to walk away from God. Make the right choice. Trust in God's infinite wisdom. Trust in God's perfect love for you. Seek God's presence in the midst of your storm.

As I study the book of Job chapter 42, I realize the importance of continuing to pray for those who hurt me; the significance of God laying a table in the presence of our enemies. We need to pray even for those who have hurt us. Let's look at the break-through that came from Job's prayer for his friends.

We must learn to intercede for other people. Here's the thing about praying for other people. When you pray for others, God has a way of blessing you! Praying for other people is like putting cologne on somebody else. You can't put some on them without getting a little on yourself!

The friends that Job was praying for were the same friends who abused, misused, and accused him. He didn't just pray for the friends who helped him, but also those who turned against him.

Anybody can pray for folks who love them back. Jesus said the world does that. Anybody can bless those who bless them. Jesus said sinners do that. But can you love your enemies? Can you do good to those who spitefully use you?

Can you bless those who curse you? Can you help those who hurt you? Can you lift those who cut you down? It is not until you learn to pray for those who despise you that your turnaround comes. I didn't say it was simple or easy.

But it's possible and necessary. If your stuff is going to turn around you must pray for those who have dogged you. May the Lord grant us the strength to be able to accomplish this. Amen. Victory comes from letting go of those who have hurt and betrayed you.

Job 42:2-17

"12 The Lord blessed the latter part of Job's life more than the former part. He had fourteen thousand sheep, six thousand camels, a thousand yoke of oxen and a thousand donkeys.

13 And he also had seven sons and three daughters.

14 The first daughter he named Jemimah, the second Keziah and the third Keren-Happuch.

15 Nowhere in all the land were there found women as beautiful as Job's daughters, and their father granted them an inheritance along with their brothers.

16 After this, Job lived a hundred and forty years; he saw his children and their children to the fourth generation.

17 And so Job died, an old man and full of years."

God always puts His best blessing at the end. At the beginning, Job was a multi-millionaire; he had houses, cattle, donkeys and land. At the end of his life God gave him twice as many sheep, oxen, cattle, donkeys, then gave him sons and daughters. All of your blessings are not financial. Some are relationships.

It was at the end of his life that Job got his greatest blessings. Because that is the type of God we serve. He always saves His best for last. It does not matter how bad your life is right now. Don't jump off a bridge. The very fact that you are here is an indication that you have not seen all of God's best. Don't give up because God saves His best for last. Wait a minute; everybody is not broke or struggling, but no matter how good it is for you now, God saves His best for last!

It is intentional, God knew He had the last move and knew how this whole journey would end. The devil does not know our end, so just hold fast unto the Lord. Every storm we go through will work out for our good. Every experience Joseph went through was for a purpose.

The brothers of Joseph were planning evil against him, but God was sending him ahead of the family to save them. The Lord knew in advance there would be famine and He made a divine provision for them. The author and finisher of your faith is always writing our story and has a way to end the story in a way that will blow the minds of people.

Chapter 3

THE SURVIVAL PACK

What does one need to survive a storm? Life jackets, lifeboats, flashlights, rhema, faith and hope, His presence.

Hope is the most important survival item in your storm – it can take you a long way. Show me anyone who has survived a storm and I will show you their hope-meter; because when you have lost your hope, you have lost everything.

My simple definition of hope is the belief that my tomorrow will be better than my today. David knew about the power of hope when life looks hopeless:

Psalm 42:1-5 (NIV)

"1 As the deer pants for streams of water,
so my soul pants for you, my God.

2 My soul thirsts for God, for the living God.
When can I go and meet with God?

3 My tears have been my food
day and night,

> while people say to me all day long,
> 'Where is your God?'
>
> 4 These things I remember
> as I pour out my soul:
> how I used to go to the house of God
> under the protection of the Mighty One
> with shouts of joy and praise
> among the festive throng.
>
> 5 Why, my soul, are you downcast?
> Why so disturbed within me?
> Put your hope in God,
> for I will yet praise him,
> my Savior and my God."

Verses 1 and 2 sounds as if everything is okay with David. But it's not. Verse three says, "My tears have been my food day and night." Life will be unbearable if your tears are your food day and night; that means you are really suffering from hopelessness and despair. As David pens this Psalm, he is depressed and his soul is discouraged.

Yet in verse 4, he shouts for joy and in verse 5 he says he is going to remember the Lord, put his hope in Him and praise Him. I will discuss more about the power of remembrance in the next chapter.

One powerful attitude or quality that can sustain any person through a storm is the ability to encourage yourself in the Lord.

If you journey through a moment when you have not received any answers from God, be still and have confidence that He will do it in due time. So talk to yourself, write to yourself, and keep a journal about your faith in God.

David encourages himself on several occasions. There are times when life crumbles, and the very friends who you thought might be there for you cannot be found; or even give you the wrong information. You are really able to identify those who love you when you are in the storm. Look at yourself in the mirror and speak God's words to yourself because there is life and death in your tongue.

In verse 5, David asks himself, "Why are you in despair, O my soul? And why have you become disturbed within me?" He doesn't deny his pain or avoid it, rather he addresses it and tells himself what to do.

What changed David's feelings of hopelessness and discouragement was focusing on God instead of the problem, and also on what God was going to do, even though he couldn't see it at the time.

Having faith in God will help you overcome any emotional despair, depression or hopelessness, tough times, battle scenes and seasons of drought.

Whose report will you believe? Have you received any unbearable news, difficult prognoses, or losses? Remember, Satan may have a "word", the doctor may have a "word", your job, friends or spouse may have a "word", but God always has the final word.

Only God can take a mess and turn it into a miracle if you put your hope in Him. He promises that "those who put their hope in Me will not be disappointed." (Isaiah 49:23 NIV)

I know your hopelessness may seem overwhelming and you may even wonder how you could ever overcome it, but strive to do as Abraham did – hope when he had no hope at all: "In hope against hope he believed." (Romans 4:18) Against all hope, Abraham in hope believed and so became the father of many nations, just as it had been said to him, "So shall your offspring be." God will honor your trust. He can turn your emotional pain into victorious gain.

The Force of Faith

One needs the force of faith to deal with the force of a storm. Let's look at Hebrews 11, which simply explains faith and lists faith champions:

Hebrews 11:1-6 (NKJV)

"1 Now faith is the substance of things hoped for, the evidence of things not seen.

2 For by it the elders obtained a good report.

3 Through faith we understand that the worlds were framed by the word of God, so that things which are seen were not made of things which do appear.

4 By faith Abel offered unto God a more excellent sacrifice than Cain, by which he obtained witness that he was righteous, God testifying of his gifts: and by it he being dead yet speaketh.

5 By faith Enoch was translated that he should not see death; and was not found, because God had translated him: for before his translation he had this testimony, that he pleased God.

6 But without faith it is impossible to please him: for he that cometh to God must believe that he is, and that he is a rewarder of them that diligently seek him."

If you read the whole chapter of Hebrews 11, you will realize that one thing that they all have in common is obedience to God even when what they were asked to do did not make sense. Guess what? Faith does not make sense!

Human reasoning and faith are opposites; or our natural mind cannot work with faith.

The just shall live by faith (Romans 1:16). Whatever Jesus did was done with faith. Faith is the way we live in the kingdom and in Luke 1:37 the Bible says, with God; all things are possible as long as there is hope and faith.

Faith feeds on the impossible, and blessed are those who have not seen but believe. Faith moves the hand of God, it's the force that can do the impossible. Faith can even cause time to slow down or speed up.

The enemy is always looking to attack your faith and wants you to come to the place where the masses are controlled with fear. The enemy is after our faith, because faith will defeat him all the time. 2 Timothy 1:7: "God has not given us the spirit of fear, but of peace, love, and a sound mind." The enemy uses fear all the time to cause us to sink, not hear, abandon our dreams, become heavy and not stay focused.

Learn to speak or confess no fear; no fear of what people will say, no fear of what will happen to you, no fear of getting sick, no fear of evil. If we can walk without fear of running out of resources, our life will change. The bolder you are, the clearer you can hear from God for divine directions.

Faith is a collaboration between your heart and your mouth.

Hebrews 10:23

"Let us hold fast the profession of our faith without wavering; for he is faithful that promised."

You are what you profess always; collaborate with your conviction so that the enemy is not able to implant any negative report or contradict your faith. The enemy mostly brings fear in our lives through what we see and hear. Whose report will you believe? During this season of Covid-19, panic and fear has been generated from TV. We need to believe the report of the Lord. Some people live their lives based on what they hear, read and Google, or their family history.

What I mean by family history is that most people have experienced diseases being passed on from one generation to the next because the cycle was not broken even after they receive Christ. The salvation package or redemption package comes with a new identity and new kingdom which does not include your family history of a particular disease.

The fact that you've been informed that everyone in this family has this particular ailment does not mean you have to accept it. Live by faith and not by sight and or by what you hear. These reports create fear; always cast fear out when it comes knocking at your door.

Let's look at Mary's visitation by Angel Gabriel:

Luke 1

"34 Then said Mary unto the angel, How shall this be, seeing I know not a man?

35 And the angel answered and said unto her, The Holy Ghost shall come upon thee, and the power of the Highest shall overshadow thee: therefore also that holy thing which shall be born of thee shall be called the Son of God.

36 And, behold, thy cousin Elisabeth, she hath also conceived a son in her old age: and this is the sixth month with her, who was called barren.

37 For with God nothing shall be impossible.

38 And Mary said, Behold the handmaid of the Lord; be it unto me according to thy word. And the angel departed from her.

39 And Mary arose in those days, and went into the hill country with haste, into a city of Juda;

40 And entered into the house of Zacharias, and saluted Elisabeth.

41 And it came to pass, that, when Elisabeth heard the salutation of Mary, the babe leaped in her womb; and Elisabeth was filled with the Holy Ghost:

42 And she spake out with a loud voice, and said, Blessed art thou among women, and blessed is the fruit of thy womb.

43 And whence is this to me, that the mother of my Lord should come to me?

44 For, lo, as soon as the voice of thy salutation sounded in mine ears, the babe leaped in my womb for joy.

45 And blessed is she that believed: for there shall be a performance of those things which were told her from the Lord.

46 And Mary said, My soul doth magnify the Lord,

47 And my spirit hath rejoiced in God my Savior.

48 For he hath regarded the low estate of his handmaiden: for, behold, from henceforth all generations shall call me blessed.

49 For he that is mighty hath done to me great things; and holy is his name."

After Angel Gabriel brought Mary's message to her, the first question she asked was: How shall this be, seeing I know not a man? In verse 35, Angel Gabriel responded to her question. Biologically, there is no way that can be possible, but Mary's response was a great confirmation of faith. Mary responded in verse 38: "And Mary said, Behold the handmaid of the Lord; be it unto me according to thy word. And the angel departed from her."

We can learn a lot from verses 48-49 on how Mary behaved right after the visitation of Angel Gabriel. Mary went to Elizabeth right away, she had not even experienced morning sickness yet but was making this powerful declaration: "For he hath regarded the low estate of his handmaiden: for, behold, from henceforth all generations shall call me blessed. 49 For he that is mighty hath done to me great things; and holy is his name." Mary acted on faith with the impossible.

To get faith

Feed your spirit – faith comes by hearing the word of God. When we eat natural food, it goes into our body, it gets broken down and we get energy for the body. When we eat the word of God, we get energy which is faith. Rhema (a word spoken to a specific individual at a specific time for a specific assignment) is needed to get through any difficult season.

Chapter 4

THE POWER OF REMEMBRANCE IN THE STORM

One of the keys to surviving every storm is to remember the miracles and power of the captain. Let's read about one of the storms that the disciples faced:

Mark 6:45-50

"45 Immediately Jesus made his disciples get into the boat and go on ahead of him to Bethsaida, while he dismissed the crowd.

46 After leaving them, he went up on a mountainside to pray.

47 Later that night, the boat was in the middle of the lake, and he was alone on land.

48 He saw the disciples straining at the oars, because the wind was against them. Shortly before dawn he went out to them, walking on the lake. He was about to pass by them,

49 but when they saw him walking on the lake, they thought he was a ghost. They cried out,

50 because they all saw him and were terrified.

Immediately he spoke to them and said, 'Take courage! It is I. Don't be afraid.'"

While on their way to Bethsaida, they faced a huge wind and were afraid. Jesus was not with them, but He knew what would happen to them and had already made provisions for escape for them. To touch on the power of remembrance, we will read in that same chapter a wonderful miracle that Jesus performed. This was a few hours before they faced the wind.

"34 When Jesus landed and saw a large crowd, he had compassion on them, because they were like sheep without a shepherd. So he began teaching them many things.

35 By this time it was late in the day, so his disciples came to him. 'This is a remote place,' they said, 'and it's already very late.

36 Send the people away so that they can go to the surrounding countryside and villages and buy themselves something to eat.'

37 But he answered, 'You give them something to eat.'

They said to him, 'That would take more than half a year's wages! Are we to go and spend that much on bread and give it to them to eat?'

38 'How many loaves do you have?' he asked. 'Go and see.'

When they found out, they said, 'Five – and two fish.'

39 Then Jesus directed them to have all the people sit down in groups on the green grass.

40 So they sat down in groups of hundreds and fifties.

41 Taking the five loaves and the two fish and looking up to heaven, he gave thanks and broke the loaves. Then he gave them to his disciples to distribute to the people. He also divided the two fish among them all.

42 They all ate and were satisfied,

43 and the disciples picked up twelve basketfuls of broken pieces of bread and fish.

44 The number of the men who had eaten was five thousand."

Jesus had performed this miracle right in front of the disciples; Jesus dismissed the multitude and then informed the disciples to go to the other side. The storm came and they had totally forgotten the power and authority which they had, and that they had just witnessed a great miracle with many baskets full of food left. The power of remembrance would have kept their faith strongly in the Lord, knowing that Jesus would see them through.

Let's now look at David:

If you can keep a diary of the many blessings, victories and testimonies obtained through the powerful hands of the most high, it will keep you going always. That was one of the weapons David used when he faced Goliath. It was his remembrance of the strength the Lord gave him to defeat the bear and lion's attacks and knowing his God.

I keep a journal and read back through my journals. Each time I do that, I realize the many ways that God has been so faithful in my life. I remember times when I felt lost and afraid, but God was actually at work in ways that I couldn't see at the time. I reminisce on how God repeatedly used painful situations to draw me into deeper intimacy with Him. Reflecting on old journals gives me a fresh perspective on current circumstances and renews my hope for the future.

"For they that know their God, they shall be strong and they shall do exploits." (Daniel 11:32)

On our Christian journey, we are bound to face Goliath, but it will take our faith in the Lord and remembering who He is. Most of the Psalms that David wrote depict his extreme remembrance of the goodness of the Lord, His mighty power, and his realization that there is nothing he has received that God did not give to him. David remembers all his victories, escapes and elevations. He ascribes all his successes to God.

"I will remember the deeds of the Lord; yes I will remember your miracles of long ago. I will consider all of your works and meditate on all your mighty deeds." (Psalm 77:11)

For he said, "you come to me with a sword, with a spear and with javelin. But I come to you in the name of the Lord of hosts, the God of the armies of Israel." (1 Samuel 17:45) God became what he called Him; the commander of heaven's army. There was no way David could have lost the battle. We have the whole of heaven on our side, we therefore cannot experience defeat.

In 1 Peter 5:7 the apostle tells us, "Cast all your anxiety on him because he cares for you."

And in Philippians 4:6 the apostle Paul wrote, "Do not be anxious about anything, but in everything, by prayer and petition, with thanksgiving, present your requests to God."

Now, let's look at Numbers 33:1-9:

"1 This is the route the Israelites followed as they marched out of Egypt under the leadership of Moses and Aaron.

2 At the Lord's direction, Moses kept a written record of their progress. These are the stages of their march, identified by the different places where they stopped along the way.

3 They set out from the city of Rameses in early spring – on the fifteenth day of the first month – on the morning after the first Passover celebration. The people of Israel left defiantly, in full view of all the Egyptians.

4 Meanwhile, the Egyptians were burying all their firstborn sons, whom the Lord had killed the night before. The Lord had defeated the gods of Egypt that night with great acts of judgment!

5 After leaving Rameses, the Israelites set up camp at Succoth.

6 Then they left Succoth and camped at Etham on the edge of the wilderness.

7 They left Etham and turned back toward Pi-hahiroth, opposite Baal-zephon, and camped near Migdol.

8 They left Pi-hahiroth and crossed the Red Sea
into the wilderness beyond. Then they traveled
for three days into the Etham wilderness and
camped at Marah.

9 They left Marah and camped at Elim, where
there were twelve springs of water and seventy
palm trees."

Life is a journey characterized by movement – detours, roller coasters, red lights, stop signs, roadwork, all of which can create a delay. No matter the delays, God will go before thee, and make the crooked places straight: "I will break in pieces the gates of brass, and cut in sunder the bars of iron." (Isaiah 45:2)

In verse 2, God instructed Moses to keep a written record of their journey. There are many reasons why God wanted the Israelites to record the starting point of the journey and all the various stops they made. Keeping record helps you measure your progress in life and develop faith and hope. Taking stock of where you are now enables you to show gratitude for the fact that, even though you have not arrived yet, you are not where you used to be.

The Israelites were not in the promised land yet, however they were not in Ramesey (Egypt) either. The Israelites saw many signs and wonders in Egypt. They witnessed the 10 plagues. At the time, there was full darkness in the whole of Egypt, but in Goshem where the Israelites lived, they had light. The Angel of Death came, but the firstborn sons of the Israelite were spared. The remembrance of these signs should give everyone hope in the Lord.

God knows that mankind can forget His goodness easily, so He urged Moses to maintain documentation of past events. On their journey to the promised land, they came to the Red Sea. For some people, the Red Sea is the end of their journey. Between you and your destiny stands a mighty Red Sea. Everyone will one day face a Red Sea. They show up in marriages, businesses, church, etc.

In front of the Israelites was this huge Red Sea, behind them was the huge Egyptian army. Let's look at what the Israelites said to Moses. This shows how human beings can easily be moved by a storm to change their mind and forget all the prior miracles they witnessed in Egypt.

Exodus 14:10-12

"10 And when Pharaoh drew near, the children of Israel lifted their eyes, and behold, the Egyptians marched after them. So they were very afraid, and the children of Israel cried out to the Lord.

11 Then they said to Moses, 'Because there were no graves in Egypt, have you taken us away to die in the wilderness? Why have you so dealt with us, to bring us up out of Egypt?

12 Is this not the word that we told you in Egypt, saying, "Let us alone that we may serve the Egyptians?" For it would have been better for us

to serve the Egyptians than that we should die in the wilderness.'

13 And Moses said to the people, 'Do not be afraid. Stand still, and see the salvation of the Lord, which He will accomplish for you today. For the Egyptians whom you see today, you shall see again no more forever.

14 The Lord will fight for you, and you shall hold your peace.'"

It was just a short journey and the Israelites had forgotten about all the miracles and promises. These were the people who had been in severe bondage; now free and on their way to the promise land. They experienced the first storm, and all of a sudden had forgotten about everything and now wished they were back serving their masters. God will always make a way through the Red Sea; if He sends you on a path, He factors in the storms on your way. He goes before you and makes every crooked path straight. Never forget His goodness, as you remember every testimony in your life; it will boost your faith and hope.

After the Red Sea experience, just 3 days later they came to Mara and guest what happened again? Let's read:

Exodus 15:22-25

"22 So Moses brought Israel from the Red Sea; then they went out into the Wilderness of Shur.

And they went three days in the wilderness and found no water.

23 Now when they came to Marah, they could not drink the waters of Marah, for they were bitter. Therefore the name of it was called Marah.

24 And the people complained against Moses, saying, 'What shall we drink?'

25 So he cried out to the Lord, and the Lord showed him a tree. When he cast it into the waters, the waters were made sweet."

In verse 24, the people complained against Moses. As you move on in life, you will come to a state of Marah (a bitter situation). Marah represents bitter times, difficult places in life; a break-up of a relationship, a betrayal, the loss of a loved one, backstabbing, the loss of a job. The people were thirsty, found water; got excited about it but it was bitter.

Have you been in a situation where you found a glimpse of light at the end of the tunnel and got there just to realize it was not a light? Have you experienced shattered hope in your life? Perhaps you've prayed for the gift of the womb, and gotten pregnant only to end up losing the baby. This is Marah. But God instructed Moses to pick a particular leaf, dip it in the water and it became sweet. The Lord will always give you the refreshment you need on your journey, just remember His miraculous hands.

Chapter 5

THE CALM AFTER THE STORM

S ometimes life feels like one has been swept away into the middle of an ocean without a compass.

Joshua 1:9

"9 Have I not commanded you? Be strong and courageous. Do not be afraid; do not be discouraged, for the Lord your God will be with you wherever you go."

God will carry you through. One of my major dramatic disruptions was the sudden death of the man I called my second father. He adopted me like his own son, loved and cared for not just me alone but my entire family. His home-calling made a huge impact in my life, "but in the year that King Uzziah died, I saw the Lord, high and exalted, seated on a throne; and the train of his robe filled the temple." (Isaiah 6:1 {NIV}).

His calling opened my eyes to be more intimate with God, there were many questions I asked God, some He answered. His ways are not our ways. The week my loved one passed, me and our prayer team were praying for him. He had requested to talk to me the day before he passed and I did.

On the day of his demise, we had a phone prayer meeting. I spoke with him and prepared for the prayer meeting for him. Almost at the end of the prayer meeting, I heard my wife crying hysterically running into my room to break the news that the hospital had called to report his death.

As a young pastor of a new church, you never plan for such an event. I was really confused for a moment. What message should I share with the family and the entire congregation? On my way to meet the spouse and daughter, I prayed to God and the spirit of the Lord directed me to encourage the family that He, Jehovah God, kept him until this time. I stayed up all night praying because I had to share the news with the church at our "Fresh Oil Morning Devotion Prayer Line."

While praying, at around 2am, I heard a voice like someone was having a conversation with me. The message was: "Nana! Shut up, the doctors gave him three months to live and I gave him 11 years; don't think I did not hear your prayers. I did, and I have called him to come and rest."

As soon as I got that message, I gathered myself and went to bed. At 5am I went on our prayer line to pray and it was obvious that the church was very heavy. I shared the message I had received from God and indeed, it elevated our church to appreciate God and to thank God for the time he spent on earth.

We celebrated him for his love, kindness and dedication to kingdom business. It was only God who gave me strength and comforted the entire church. You are really able to identify those who love you when you are in the storm.

Your storm might be infertility or the loss of a job which can create both physical and emotional challenges. Or it may be a divorce, suspension from a school, failing an exam, an accident or maybe an addiction.

Let's look at the life of Noah, and his life after the storm:

Genesis 8:6-11, 15-22

"6 After forty days Noah opened a window he had made in the ark

7 and sent out a raven, and it kept flying back and forth until the water had dried up from the earth.

8 Then he sent out a dove to see if the water had receded from the surface of the ground.

9 But the dove could find nowhere to perch because there was water over all the surface of the earth; so it returned to Noah in the ark. He reached out his hand and took the dove and brought it back to himself in the ark.

10 He waited seven more days and again sent out the dove from the ark.

11 When the dove returned to him in the evening, there in its beak was a freshly plucked olive leaf! Then Noah knew that the water had receded from the earth."

"15 Then God said to Noah,

16 'Come out of the ark, you and your wife and your sons and their wives.

17 Bring out every kind of living creature that is with you – the birds, the animals, and all the creatures that move along the ground – so they can multiply on the earth and be fruitful and increase in number on it.'

18 So Noah came out, together with his sons and his wife and his sons' wives.

19 All the animals and all the creatures that move along the ground and all the birds – everything that moves on land – came out of the ark, one kind after another.

20 Then Noah built an altar to the Lord and, taking some of all the clean animals and clean birds, he sacrificed burnt offerings on it.

21 The Lord smelled the pleasing aroma and said in his heart: 'Never again will I curse the ground because of humans, even though every inclination of the human heart is evil from childhood. And never again will I destroy all living creatures, as I have done.

22 As long as the earth endures, seedtime and harvest, cold and heat, summer and winter, day and night will never cease.'"

1. *Trials do not mean God is judging you.*
God chose Noah and his family out of the millions of people on earth to build an ark and to preserve a remnant of humanity to repopulate the world. Noah responded to God in faith and for that reason, God preserved him and his family.

2. *God often takes me through trials rather than removing me from them.*
According to Genesis 8:6-11, 16-22, God did not spare Noah from all of the devastating effects of the flood. Though Noah faithfully did everything God had commanded him, he still had to go through those storms and start life all over again in the midst of some horrific conditions.

What God did was sustain Noah and his family throughout those trials. He warned Noah about the judgment to come and provided a way for him to be able to survive in the midst of the storm by building the ark.

God is more than capable of removing His people from trials and sometimes He does do that. We often see God working this way throughout the Bible and in our lives today. We certainly see this with many of the healings that Jesus performed in His earthly ministry.

Shadrach, Meshach and Abednego had to endure the fiery furnace, but God was present with them in the furnace and brought them through it. If this had happened in today's church, the church and the community would have judged them, believing it was probably their sin that led them into the furnace.

Daniel was not spared from the lion's den, but God did protect him while he was there. In our time, the masses would probably have judged him.

Let's consider the young blind man who was healed by Jesus Christ in John 9:1-7.

"1 As he went along, he saw a man blind from birth.

2 His disciples asked him, 'Rabbi, who sinned, this man or his parents, that he was born blind?'

3 'Neither this man nor his parents sinned,' said Jesus, 'but this happened so that the works of God might be displayed in him.

4 As long as it is day, we must do the works of him who sent me. Night is coming, when no one can work.

5 While I am in the world, I am the light
of the world.'

6 After saying this, he spit on the ground, made
some mud with the saliva, and put it
on the man's eyes.

7 'Go,' he told him, 'wash in the Pool of Siloam'
[this word means "Sent"]. So the man went and
washed, and came home seeing.

- The disciples questioned Jesus in verse 2, "Rabbi, who sinned?" Society will always conclude and have their opinion about you, but God has the final say. Always do right by God; understand that even though we may walk through the darkest valley, we should not fear any evil, for the Lord is with us.

Jesus ordered the storm to be still. Peace is always greater than the storm.

In the midst of the storm, try to give your entire attention to what God is doing, and don't get worked up about what may or may not happen tomorrow. God will help you deal with whatever hard things come up when the time comes.

In one of Smith Wigglesworth's readings about his faith and spiritual exploits, he shared an encounter with the devil: "We were sleeping one night, when the manifestation of evil filled the room and the spirit of fear gripped both of us. Polly was so frightened she could not open her eyes. I suddenly sat up, in the bed, and saw the devil. I rubbed my eyes to be sure, it was him. I said, 'Oh! It's only you.' I then turned to Polly and told her to go back to sleep, it was nothing of consequence, and I laid my head back down. Suddenly an overwhelming sense of peace and love filled the room and we had the most blessed sleep ever."

In the middle of the storms of life, learn to let Jesus be your peace factor. If He did it for Smith Wigglesworth, He will do it for us too.

The storm brings the rain:

All things will work together for our good. The devil meant it for evil, but God meant it for good. Every season is temporary; the key to life is outlasting the season. If you can stay warm enough, summer will soon come. A crisis is something you cannot control, so understand it will pass away.

Crises have always been sources of development and growth. A man was advised by his wife for years to maintain his weight and live a healthy lifestyle. This man never listened to his wife until one day he was admitted to the hospital and tests revealed that most of his arteries were clogged and he was at a serious risk of a heart attack. Guess what? He changed overnight. Sometimes a crisis is the only way we learn to make changes.

A storm or fire may destroy a whole forest, but after it begins to regrow, the new forest is always better than the previous one. A friend of mine lives in a flood zone; he needed many repairs in his house and money was tight. He did have flood insurance on the house. During Hurricane Sandy, his house was severely damaged. His family had to stay in a hotel for months until the insurance repaired his house. During the repairs, all the damage that was there before the storm also got fixed. When it was all said and done, he got a beautifully renovated house which was much better the one he had before with an even nicer landscape. It was a difficult experience, but it worked out well for him and his family.

A crisis creates an opportunity for creativity and also invents new ways to deal with future crises.

The eagle is the king of all birds; it has one of the longest, strongest and biggest wings but its life begins as a small egg. The only way the eaglet learns to fly is for the mother to fly very high with the eaglet and then leave it to fall. The eaglets have two choices, to learn to fly or fall and die. Every crisis is meant to teach, test our faith in the Lord and strengthen us in a way that the enemy will have no clue about. Faith is believing in the midst of the dark (crisis) what God told you in the light (when things were good). Do you believe during winter that summer will surely come? Then believe that this too shall pass.

John 16:33

"I have told you these things, so that in me you may have peace. In this world you will have trouble. But take heart! I have overcome the world."

A crisis is able to turn enemies into friends. It creates unity in a community or country, it produces empathy. God sometimes allows us to see darkness so that we can appreciate the light.

After 9/11, the whole of New York city and county came together to support each other. The Covid-19 pandemic also brought the world together to a large extent, taught the world a lot, deflated pride and even made a lot of people turn to God for help.

Storms sometimes remove pollutants and get certain people out of your life. There are friends who will be with you in the storm and also when the storm is over. Storms are usually not the issue because they will always come. When they come, they test what we are made of. The structure is more important than the storm.

One of the best ways to face a storm with joy is to remember God's goodness.

Keys to living above the storm:

- The eagle is able to fly above the storm because it believes in itself. Believe you are built for the storm.
- Don't curse the storm; you can use it to your benefit. Businesses have been created in the midst of a storm.
- When the storm comes, it means that God knows you can bear it. God knew Job would be able to get through his crisis.

Let's look at the Covid-19 pandemic as a case study for us to learn about God's purpose before and after the storm. What did Noah experience after he came out of the ark?

The lockdown and social distancing prevented a lot of people from constantly running around or driving to many different places. This lowered air pollution, rivers are cleaning up, vegetation and wildlife are returning to areas in which they haven't been seen for a long time. I believe Noah also experienced a similar situation.

Noah and his family were in the ark for 40 days; it was a great time for the family to bond. The forced isolation during the Covid-19 season served as a reminder of how much our loved ones mean to us.

And with this newfound importance of connection, families are coming together in ways like never before such as eating at the table together and praying together.

Surely you can see God has not forsaken us.

This stormy season has made us realize we are all equal. Rich or poor, great or small, this Covid-19 virus has impacted all of us. The proportion of this pandemic clearly proved that we are all one big world.

The storm has taught us a lot of lessons, such as the importance of stocking up on non-perishable foods or items and emergency supplies, having emergency funds and maintaining personal hygiene. Many people are starting new businesses, investing and having a more diversified portfolio, while companies are adopting a system in which some employees are working from home. Last but not least, we have learned not to put all our eggs in one basket.

As I get ready to end this chapter and this book, I would like to say thank you for reading along. Let's take another look at what God told Noah and how God used 8 people to replenish the earth. God blessed Noah and his family.

Genesis 8:15-17, 20

"15 Then God said to Noah,

16 'Come out of the ark, you and your wife and your sons and their wives.

17 Bring out every kind of living creature that is with you – the birds, the animals, and all the creatures that move along the ground – so they can multiply on the earth and be fruitful and increase in number on it.'

20 Then Noah built an altar to the Lord and, taking some of all the clean animals and clean birds, he sacrificed burnt offerings on it.

In verse 20, Noah built an altar and made an offering to the Lord after leaving the ark. God blessed Noah and his sons and told them to repopulate and fill the earth. Building an altar and burning an offering indicates Noah's gratitude to the Lord God Almighty for preserving his family.

The altar also served as a memorial; always keep records of the blessings of the Lord. Thanksgiving moves the hand of God; it multiplies whatever you have in your hands. Whenever God becomes pleased with your sacrifice of praise, worship and thanksgiving, He will always bless you. When the Lord smelled the pleasing aroma of Noah's burnt offering, He made a vow. Let your gratitude cause God to make a vow concerning you and your family. Amen…

Today is May 31st 2020; I was done writing this book about a week ago. I had been creating a series on "Bouncing Back" which focuses on how to deal with the Covid-19 crisis. While preparing my sermon for Sunday services, the Lord directed me to share a message on "Who is your anchor." I started putting my message together and I felt this strong push to include this message in the book.

Who is your Anchor?

GENERAL DEFINITION: An anchor is a device normally made of metal that is used to connect a vessel to the bed of a body of water to prevent the craft from drifting due to wind or current.

No sailor needs an anchor when the waters are calm, but when weather conditions change and become dangerous, an anchor becomes essential.

The issues of this world are like a wavy sea; restless, unstable and scary. Like a ship in a storm, we can be tossed and be driven by wind. Through it all, God has made provision for his people to be delivered from the storms of life. He's provided an anchor so strong that no storm can stand it.

In life, most of the people you come across who are driven helplessly by circumstances tend to be miserable due to lack of a support system or an anchor. An anchor brings comfort, peace and confidence to the captain of the ship because it gives them some assurance that they will survive whenever they face any storm.

Imagine a sailor sailing almost to the port of his destination and being hit by a sudden strong wind which could blow the ship back to its departing area if there were no anchors to keep it in place.

A wise captain will say, "We've gotten this far and we're not going to be driven back and lose time. Throw down the anchor and let's hold this spot!"

The safety of the crew on a ship is heavily dependent on the anchor, therefore they cannot be made of just any kind of metal, but must be of a tough, heavy and compact material which will bear all the strain that is likely to come upon it at the worst of times and also able to resist the corrosive power of saltwater.

Our anchor, which is made up of God's promise and the assurance of our salvation, secures our lives. God never goes back on His promises and He keeps them from one generation to the other. This anchor is our Lord Jesus who died on the cross to save us, resurrected, ascended to heaven and now sitting at the right hand of the Father interceding on our behalf. If God can allow His only son to die for us, why wouldn't He give us all things when we ask and also anchor us in a storm?

What is the use of an anchor at the seabed when the cable connecting it is very weak?

The anchor may grip the seabed, but the cable connecting it to the ship must be able to withstand the pull. The last thing you need is the risk of a cable breakage in a storm. The cable is our faith and the anchor is our hope. Never lose your faith; never.

When storms hit a ship, the force of the wind only drives the anchor deeper into the seabed. The more the ship drags, the tighter the anchor's hold becomes. By the same token, when we face storms, they force us deeper into the things of God – and what the devil means for evil actually turns into good. We always need the presence of God.

Sometimes the storm might create fear and you might want to give up, but rely on His strength and divine direction. The anchor does not deliver us from problems but will save us from the peril. We have an anchor that cannot be moved, and He is the Lord Almighty!

REFERENCES

Cook, A; 2011; "The Unexpected Storm"; *Godtube;* viewed 13th January 2021 <https://www.godtube. com/watch/?v=DLWKLWNX>

Herring, H; 2018; "7 Things to Do When Facing the Storms of Life"; *Harold Herring.com;* viewed 13th January 2021 <https://haroldherring.com/blogs/ harolds-blogs/richthoughts/1433-7-things-to-do-when-facing-the-storms-of-life>

History.com; 2020; "September 11 Attacks"; *History;* viewed 13th January 2021; <https://www.history.com/ topics/21st-century/9-11-attacks>

Oxford English Dictionary; Oxford University Press; 2012

OTHER PUBLICATION

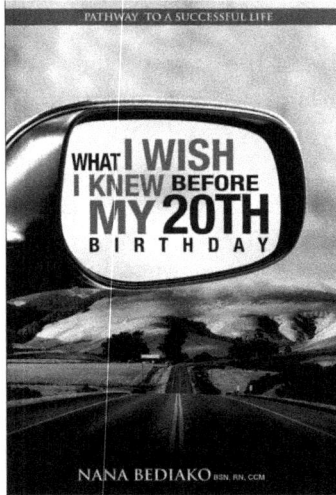

PATHWAY TO A SUCCESSFUL LIFE

WHAT I WISH I KNEW BEFORE MY 20TH BIRTHDAY

NANA BEDIAKO BSN, RN, CCM

AVAILABLE WORLDWIDE

Connect with author: